IN A WORLD CONSUMED
BY ITS OWN GREED,
THE SKIES WEEP WITH SMOG .
AF414146
AIR QUALITY TODAY
=
DANGEROUS
IT'S GETTING WORSE
EVERY DAY ...
I MISS THE STARS
WE'RE SEEING
MORE CASES EVERY WEEK .
WE CAN'T KEEP UP
skip a straw
save the planet
THE EARTH, CHOKING
ON THE REMNANTS OF
HUMAN CARELESSNESS .

IF WE'RE RIGHT, THIS COULD REVOLUTIONIZE CLEAN ENERGY
ELLEN, THIS COULD BE THE BREAKTHROUGH WE NEED
CAREFUL . . .
THIS COMPOUND IS HIGHLY VOLATILE . . .
TOGETHER, WE'LL CHANGE THE WORLD, LEO .
ON THE BRINK OF DISCOVERY, HOPE FLICKERS IN THE DARKNESS

THERE MUST BE A WAY TO STABILIZE THE REACTION.
CATALYST STABILLITY REMAINS THE KEY. POTENTIAL SOLUTIONS . . .
ENOUGH FOR TONIGHT. TOMORROW IS ANOTHER DAY
IN THE SILENCE OF NIGHT, A RESTLESS MIND SEEKS SOLACE IN DREAMS.
IN THE DEPTHS OF SLEEP, THE SUBCONSCIOUS WEAVES ITS TALES.

THAT'S IT!
CAN IT REALLY BE THIS SIMPLE?
A NEW CATALYST STRUCTURE!
INSPIRED BY A DREAM . . .
ONLY A FEW HOURS UNTIL DAWN . . .
NO TIME TO LOSE .
IN THE QUIET HOURS OF THE MORNING, A NEW HOPE DAWNS.
click

ELLEN, IF THIS WORKS, WE COULD BE ON THE VERGE OF A CLEAN ENERGY REVOLUTION
LET'S HOPE YOUR MIDNIGHT EPPIPHANY PAYS OFF, LEO
IT'S WORKING, ELLEN! THE READINGS ARE OFF THE CHARTS!
LEO, LOOK OUT!
BOOM!
IN PUTSUIT OF A DREAM, A NIGHTMARE UNFOLDS

WHERE AM I?
BEEP
BEEP
ELLEN?
WHAT IS THIS FEELING?
LIKE ENERGY FLOWING THROUGH MY VEINS . . .
DOCTOR PHI! YOU'RE AWAKE . . .
BUT HOW?
MY WIFE, DR. SKYE, WHERE IS SHE?
IS SHE ALRIGHT?
SHE'S IN A COMA, DR. PHI.
THE DOCTORS . . . THEY'RE NOT SURE IF SHE'LL MAKE IT.

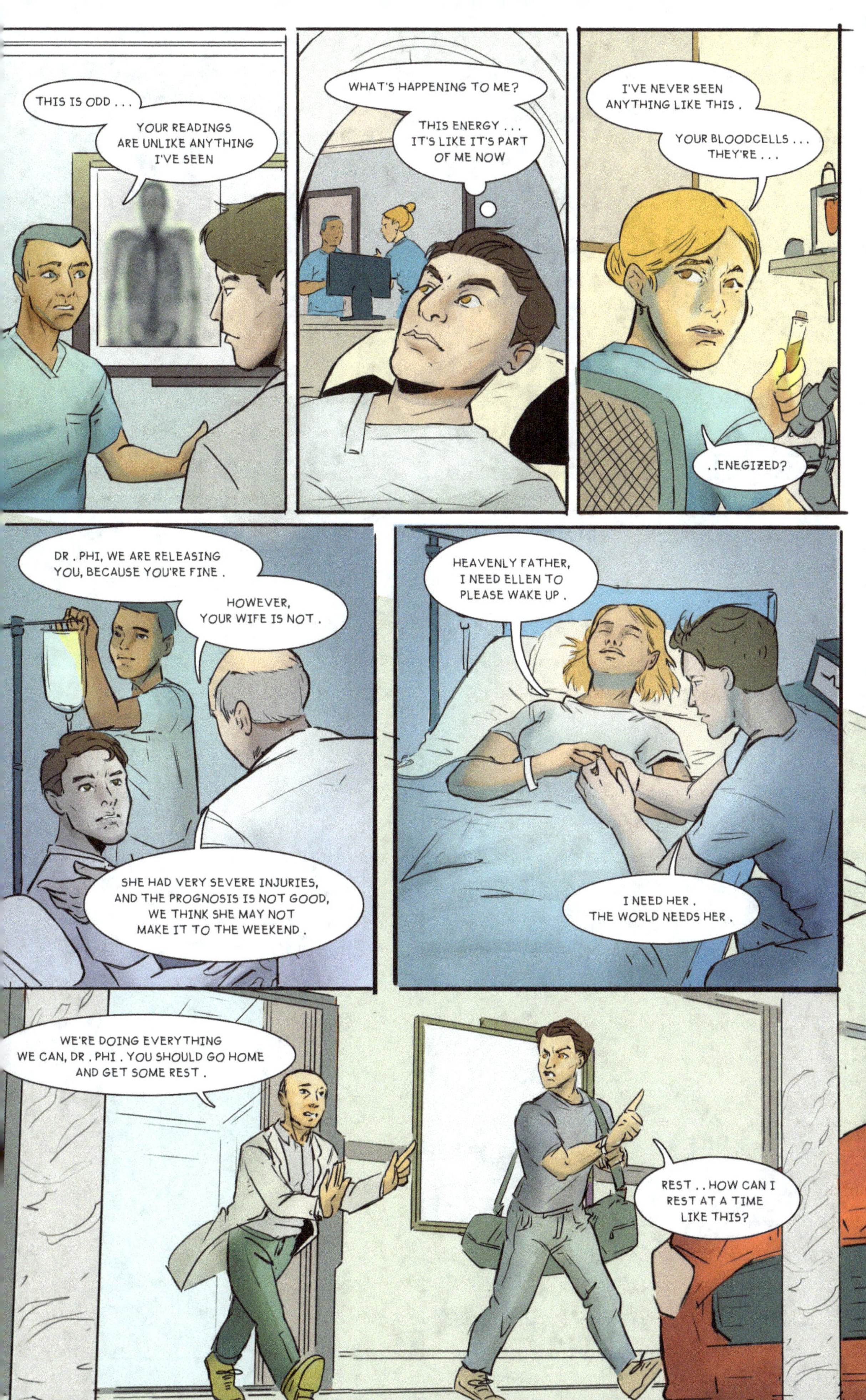

THIS IS ODD . . .
YOUR READINGS ARE UNLIKE ANYTHING I'VE SEEN
WHAT'S HAPPENING TO ME?
THIS ENERGY . . . IT'S LIKE IT'S PART OF ME NOW
I'VE NEVER SEEN ANYTHING LIKE THIS .
YOUR BLOODCELLS . . . THEY'RE . . .
. . ENEGIZED?
DR . PHI, WE ARE RELEASING YOU, BECAUSE YOU'RE FINE .
HOWEVER, YOUR WIFE IS NOT .
SHE HAD VERY SEVERE INJURIES, AND THE PROGNOSIS IS NOT GOOD, WE THINK SHE MAY NOT MAKE IT TO THE WEEKEND .
HEAVENLY FATHER, I NEED ELLEN TO PLEASE WAKE UP .
I NEED HER . THE WORLD NEEDS HER .
WE'RE DOING EVERYTHING WE CAN, DR . PHI . YOU SHOULD GO HOME AND GET SOME REST .
REST . . HOW CAN I REST AT A TIME LIKE THIS?

THIS CAN'T BE HAPPENINING . . .
NOT TO ELLEN . . . NOT TO US . . .

MAYBE . . . MAYBE I CAN FIND SOME ANSWERS HERE .

I CAN CONTROL IT . . .
SHAPE IT . . .
IT'S LIKE IT'S A PART OF ME NOW

WHAT? ! ENEGY CONVERSION!
MAYBE THIS COULD BE HARNESSED SOMEHOW!

I SHOULD TRY AND CONTAIN ALL THAT IS HAPPENING IN ME TO BETTER PROTECT EVERYTHING AND EVERYONE AROUND ME

THIS IS INCREDIBLE . . . I'M GENERATING ENORMOUS AMOUNTS OF AIR . . . AND IT'S INCREASING WITH MY EMOTIONS
IF I COULD CHANNEL MOST OF THIS AIR . . . MAYBE THROUGH A SUIT . . .
I COULD FLY!
THIS CHEST PIECE . . . IT'LL BE THE CORE . AND THE SUIT, IT NEEDS TO BE AGILE, YET STRONG
ELLEN ALWAYS HAD AN EYE FOR DETAIL . . . I'LL NEED THAT NOW.
FROM GRIEF AND HOPE, A HERO'S ARMOR BEGINS TO TAKE SHAPE

THE CENTER CHEST PIECE . . . IT MUST HARNESS AND ENHANCE MY ABILITIES .
AI INTEGRATION FOR REAL TIME MANAGEMENT . . .
ELLEN'S SEWING MACHINE FOR THE STITCHING .
THESE BOOTS WILL NEED PRECISE CONTROL . . .
VECTOR BASED CONTROLS FOR STABILITY .
A SOLITARY FIGURE, SURROUNDED BY THE TOOLS OF TRANSFORMATION .
AND A SHIELD . . . NOT JUST FOR DEFENSE,
BUT A SYMBOL OF MY MISSION .

THIS SHOULD BE ENOUGH . . .
. . . THE RUBBER WILL ENSURE IT IS AIRTIGHT, AND THE POLYESTER WILL PROTECT THE SUIT FROM THE UV RAYS .
IF I INTEGRATE THE AI WITH THE CHEST PIECE'S SENSORS, IT COULD ADJUST THE THRUST IN REAL TIME . . .
THE KEVLAR WILL PROVIDE THE PSI STRENGTH . . .
THE AI NEEDS TO MANAGE ME AND THE SUIT'S SYSTEMS . . . AND KEEP ME SAFE .
DINESH, IT'S LEO! I NEED YOUR EXPERTISE ON A PROJECT . . . SOMETHING GROUNDBREAKING .
LEO! IT'S BEEN TOO LONG . WHAT'S YOUR PROJECT ABOUT?
I'M BUILDING SOMETHING . . . A SUIT THAT COULD CHANGE THE FUTURE OF ENERGY AND MOBILITY . I NEED AN HIGH FUNCTIONING AI, YOUR SKILLS COULD MAKE IT A REALITY .
YOU'VE GOT MY ATTENTION, LEO . LET'S MAKE IT HAPPEN .

FOR STRENGTH . . . FOR ELLEN . . . FOR US ALL .
THIS CHEST CAGE . . . IT'S WHERE IT ALL COMES TOGETHER .
PERFECT TIMING, NOW, THE REAL WORK BEGINS .
WITH PRECISION AND CARE . . . A HERO'S ARMOR TAKES SHAPE
ELLEN'S TOUCH . . . IT'S PART OF THIS TOO,
EVERY PIECE . . . A STEP CLOSER TO MAKING A DIFFERENCE,

EVERY SEAM, EVERY STITCH, MUST BE PERFECT! CAN'T HAVE ANY LEAKS.
A PERFECT FIT. ELLEN WOULD HAVE BEEN PROUD.
LIKE STEPPING INTO THE FUTURE . . .
MY FUTURE .
MY FLIGHT CONTROLS ARE WORKING WELL! THIS IS INCREDIBLE!
YEEE-HAW! IT'S WORKING! I'M REALLY FLYING!
WHAT AN AMAZING NEW BEGINNING . . . AND FOR ME, A NEW MISSION .

WHAT IS THIS? ... WHO IS THIS!? I CAN ... FEEL THEIR INTENTIONS? SEE THEIR ACTIONS?
I CAN SEE IT ... THE POLLUTION.
THE PERSON RESPONSIBLE AND WHERE IT'S HAPPENING! BUT HOW?
I HAVE TO STOP THIS ... WHATEVER IT IS, IT'S GUIDING ME THERE .
WHAT DO YOU THINK YOU'RE DOING? I DO YOU UNDERSTAND THE HARM YOU'RE CAUSING?
I ... I DIDN'T THINK ANYONE WOULD SEE ...
GONK
IT'S NOT ABOUT BEING SEEN BY PEOPLE . IT'S ABOU WHAT DOESN'T POISON!

LET'S SEE WHAT THE WORLD'S UP TO TODAY . . .
BREAKING NEWS: A MYSTERIOUS FLYING MAN WAS SPOTTED LAST NIGHT, TACKLING POLLUTION, HEAD-ON IN OUR CITY!
THAT'S--
THAT'S ME! BUT HOW DID THEY !?
AS THE SUN RISES, AND SO DOES A NEW HERO IN THE PUBLIC'S EYE
IT'S LIKE A SUPERHERO FROM THE COMICS, BUT REAL! HE'S EXACTLY WHAT WE NEED!
A SYMBOL OF HOPE, HUH? MAYBE THIS IS MY CALLING . . . ELLEN, I HOPE THIS IS FOR US

THIS IS
DR. PHI...
DR. PHI,
IT'S ABOUT YOUR
WIFE...I'M AFRAI
SHE'S TAKEN A
TURN FOR THE
WORSE
HOLD ON,
ELLEN, I'M
COMING
PLEASE...
SAVE HER, PLEASE
IN MOMENTS OF DESPAIR,
EVEN HEROES FEEL THE
THREAT OF LOSS
THE JOURNEY HOME, A PATH
PAVED WITH UNCERTAINTY
AND HEARTACHE
WE'RE
DOING ALL WE CAN,
DR. PHI--
SHE'S A
FIGHTER

BENEATH THE CITY'S PULSE LIES AN EMERGING HEART OF DARKNESS, BEATING TO THE RHYTHM OF NEFARIOUS INTENT
A SYMPHONY OF CORRUPTION PLAYS WITHIN, A PRELUDE TO DISASTER ORCHESTRATED BY ONE MAN
THE PREPARATIONS ARE NEARLY COMPLETE
SOON, THE CITY WILL AWAKEN TO A NEW ERA! ONE SHAPED BY MY VISION!
EVERY SCREEN, A WINDOW TO DESTRUCTION . EVERY DIAL, A COUNTDOWN TO DOOM
THE TIME IS NOW, AND IT BEGINS TODAY! OUR MOMENT OF TRIUMPH APPROACHES . LET THE CITY TREMBLE AT THE MIGHT OF MIASMOX!

AS DAWN BREAKS, A SHADOW FALLS OVER THE CITY, A PRECURSOR TO THE TERROR THAT IS ABOUT TO UNFOLD...
LET THE CLEANSING BEGIN. THE CITY WILL BOW TO THE MIGHT OF NATURE'S WRATH, BY MY HAND!
UNBELIEVABLE! MIASMOX'S MADNESS MUST BE STOPPED. BUT ELLEN... I CAN'T LOSE HER NOW
PHASE TWO INITIATED. THE CITY WILL SOON BE OURS
WHAT'S HAPPENING!? IT'S HARD TO BREATHE!
FOR ELLEN! FOR THE CITY, FOR THE FUTURE! THIS GUY MIASMOX'SREIGN OF TERROR ENDS TONIGHT

THIS WAY, FOLKS! WE'VE GOT SHELTERS READY! STAY CALM AND FOLLOW THE SIGNS!
NEIGHBOR HELP POINT
STICK TOGETHER! WE'VE GOT WATER, MASKS, EVERYTHING YOU NEED RIGHT HERE!
THERE ... THE WAREHOUSE DISTRICT . THAT'S WHERE THE HEART OF THIS DARKNESS BEATS
I CAN SEE THEM ... THE PERPETRATORS, SPREADING THEIR POISON
THIS GIFT ... IT'S A BURDEN AND A BEACON . TIME TO FOLLOW THE LIGHT
FOR EVERY SHADOW CAST BY WRONGDOING, THERE WILL BE LIGHT . MY LIGHT

IT'S TIME. NO MORE HIDING, NO MORE WAITING.
WITH RESOLVE AS HIS GUIDE, MR. HYDROGEN TAKES TO THE SKIES, A BEACON OF HOPE IN THE DIM MORNING LIGHT.
THIS IS IT. MIASMOX MUST BE INSIDE.
SO! DR. HYDROGEN. YOU'RE TOO LATE. NOTHING CAN STOP ME NOW!
IT'S MR. HYDROGEN! AND IT'S YOU WHO'S TOO LATE.
A DANCE OF DESTRUCTION AND DEFENSE UNFOLDS, WITH MR. HYDROGEN'S RESOLVE TESTED AT EVERY TURN.
FOR THE EARTH!
NO! . . . THIS CANNOT BE!
GREAT WORK, MR. HYDROGEN. THE CITY OWES YOU A DEBT.
I DID WHAT HAD TO BE DONE.

THIS BATTLE WAS WON, BUT I SEE THIS STRUGGLE WILL CONTINUE .
WE SAW WHAT HAPPENED . HOW CAN WE HELP? !
IF WE COME TOGETHER, WE CAN CLEAN UP AND BETTER PROTECT OUR CITY .
EVERY PIECE OF TRASH REMOVED IS A SMALL VICTORY AND LET'S FIGURE OUT HOW TO TACKLE THE LARGER PROBLEMS
MR . HYDROGEN, WHAT MESSAGE DO YOU HAVE FOR THE CITY?
WE EACH HAVE A RESPONSIBILITY TO BETTER PROTECT OUR FAMILY OUR HOME, AND THE FUTURE . WHETHER IT'S IN THE LAND, IN THE AIR, THE WATER, OUR CLOTHES OR OUR FOOD .
LET'S UNITE AGAINST POLLUTION .
THANK YOU, MR . HYDROGEN! YOU'RE A REAL HERO!
AS MR . HYDROGEN SOARS AWAY, HIS MESSAGE RESONATES WITH THE HEARTS AND MINDS OF THOSE HE'S TOUCHED .

LAST NIGHT'S VICTORY FEELS HOLLOW . . . WITH ELLEN'S CONDITION UNCHANGED .

CHARLIE, LET'S GO SEE ELLEN . I'M SURE SHE'D WANT TO SEE YOU, ONE MORETIME .

YOU ALWAYS KNOW HOW TO MAKE HER DAY!

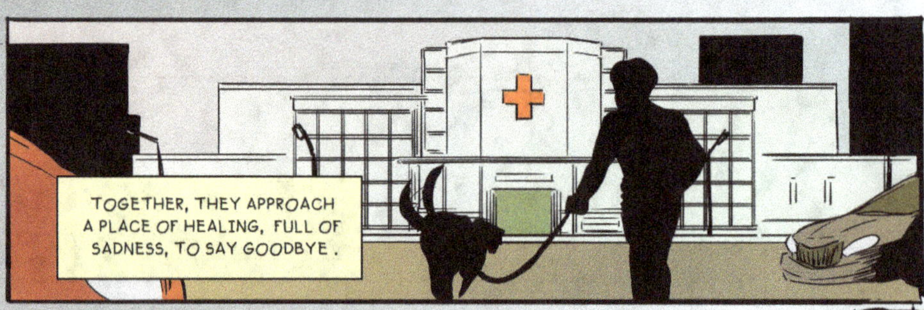

TOGETHER, THEY APPROACH A PLACE OF HEALING, FULL OF SADNESS, TO SAY GOODBYE .

GOOD TO SEE YOU, DR . PHI . AND CHARLIE, TOO GO RIGHT AHEAD .

LET'S GIVE HER THE BEST GOODBYE WE CAN .
THERAPY DOG

EASY, CHARLIE . . . LET'S NOT DISTURB HER .
IN MOMENTS OF DESPAIR, THE COMFORT OF A LOYAL FRIEND SPEAKS VOLUMES .
ELLEN, MY LOVE . . . I'M SO SORRY .
UNSEEN BY GRIEVING EYES, A MIRACLE UNFOLDS, WEAVING THE FABRIC OF HOPE FROM DESPAIR .
GOOD-BYE . I LOVE YOU .
COUGH
ELLEN?
WHAT . . . HAPPENED? WHERE AM I?
ELLEN! YOU'RE BACK! YOU'RE REALLY BACK!

ELLEN, YOU'VE MADE AN INCREDIBLE RECOVERY . I SUGGEST YOU AND DR . PHI TAKE A FEW MONTHS OFF TO FULLY RECUPERATE .
I CAN'T WAIT TO GET AWAY FROM ALL THIS, AND GO SEE OUR SON .
WHAT A GREAT IDEA . JUST YOU, ME, AND CHARLIE .
SO, MR . HYDROGEN, READY TO SHARE MORE ABOUT YOUR NEW ABILITIES ON THIS FLIGHT?
THERE'S SO MUCH TO TELL YOU, ELLEN . STARTING WITH HOW YOUR COURAGE INSPIRED ME .
AS THEY SOAR INTO THE CLOUDS, DR . PHI AND DR . SKYE EMBRACE A FUTURE FILLED WITH ADVENTURE, LOVE, AND THE UNKNOWN .